Your Spiritual Home Field Advantage: A Book About Life in the Physical World

7 Critical Mistakes People Commonly Make While Living in the Physical World... And How to Avoid Them

by Dr. Lisa Brabo and Dr. Debi Yohn

Illustrations by Sophie Everiss, The Image Refinery

Light of Change, Los Angeles, California

Your Spiritual Home Field Advantage:
A Book About Life in the Physical World

ISBN 978-0-6151-5513-5

www.lightofchange.com

Dedicated to all those among us
who step up courageously
to live open-hearted lives.

Enhance Your Life with Products from Light of Change

Products can be purchased on the Light of Change website:
www.lightofchange.com/store.htm

GUIDED SELF-HYPNOSIS CDs

These self-hypnosis recordings use the technique of progressive relaxation to guide you to a deep meditative state conducive to healing and growth.

There are four separate series of self-hypnosis CDs, as follows:

- **Adventures for the Body and Soul**
  Grab your traveling bags as you set out on adventures around the globe, and beyond. Use these rich experiences to help you grow.

- **There's No Place Like Home**
  Grief is many-layered for those who have lost a loved one. Equally layered are our feelings if we are in the process of losing someone close to us or are on the verge of transitioning Home ourselves. These meditations are designed to re-frame and ease the experience.

- **It's a Family Affair**
  Parenting is one of the most challenging and rewarding experiences that exists on this planet. Likewise, our children's lives of growing up and maturing in today's world are equally challenging and rewarding. Use these meditations to reduce the challenge and increase the reward.

- **Feeling Good is Feeling Good**
  This way to a better-feeling life.

Enhance Your Life with Products from Light of Change

Products can be purchased on the Light of Change website:
www.lightofchange.com/store.htm

ANGEL LIGHT COMMUNICATION BOARD

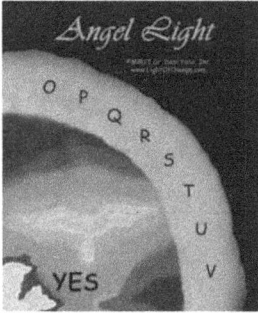

Communicate with your angels and spirit guides…

Learn about your life and your journey…

Find relief… Be happier!

Angel Light is a communication tool that helps you connect spiritually. You can gain a better understanding of your life and your journey through the profound information provided.

Many have found relief in the information they've received. Others have described heartfelt joy. And still others have experienced a strengthening of their intuitive senses through the use of Angel Light.

Contents

Introduction

Two Key Concepts Explained

You don't need to know much about sports to understand this book. We make several references to football, soccer and other games, but these are incidental to the stories in which we talk about them.

However, to help you get the most out of your reading, we should probably explain two metaphors that pop up time and again.

First, we talk a lot about "third base." This is a reference to the game of baseball — third base is the third canvas bag a runner must touch to be able to get back to "home plate" and score a point.

The defensive player who guards third base is called the third baseman. It's his job to field balls that are hit to him, and to try to keep runners on the other team from reaching third base safely.

Confused? It's OK.

The important thing to remember about third base, at least as far as this book is concerned, is this — if you try to make sense of baseball by only looking at third, you'll be lost.

We use third base in this book to describe what happens when you focus only on the physical world. If you're not broadening your perspective and looking at what's happening in the spiritual world too, it's like watching baseball by only looking at third base. The third baseman might be interesting to watch, but you'll have no idea what's happening in the larger game.

The other concept we frequently refer to is "home field advantage." This is an important one to understand.

In team sports, the team playing at their own stadium or arena is known as the home team. Their opponents are often called the visiting team, or the "away" team.

What you call the teams, however, is less important than a unique social phenomenon that seems to happen at home — often, teams seem to play better simply *because* they're at home.

Think about why this happens — the home team's stadium or arena is typically full of their own fans! Sure, some of the visiting team's fans may have come to the game to cheer on their favorites, but their numbers are usually much less than the home-team die-hards.

Not to mention things like cheerleaders, light shows, and announcers... All of these are designed to support the home team as well.

We say in the book that you have a "spiritual" home field advantage. We won't get into what that means here — after all, we want you to keep reading — but it's enough to know for now that you have fans and cheerleaders supporting your every decision, rooting for you every day.

Read on to learn more!

Chapter 1

Mistake #1 —
Underestimating the Power of
Love and Connection

Do you live life for the love of it?

Do you act differently towards those you feel connected to, as compared to those to whom you don't?

How does being loved and cared for affect you?

Do you feel there is "power" in love and connection?

Do love and connection "empower" you?

～

Johnny's New Book

"Read me this one, Daddy."

Doug read, "This is the story of the universe. It is the story of the sun, and the moon, and the stars." Johnny smiled. He

*particularly liked stars, just as he particularly liked trucks,
books, and flashlights. "Quite diverse tastes for a little boy
who became three today," Doug thought.*

*He turned the page to a deep red and gold design. The
colors shimmered even in the bedtime light of the room.
Doug continued reading, "This is love. Love is what existed
before the birth of the world."*

*"What?" Doug thought. He turned to the next page and
found the same deep red and gold. It glowed in the middle
with light like a lit candle. He sat transfixed as a ball of light
formed in the center of light and floated across the page.*

*He read, "This is how the world was formed. From love to
love. Each a part of the other."*

*Johnny laughed and pointed to the floating ball of light. Doug
couldn't believe it. Where had this book come from?*

*He turned the page again. More balls of light were forming,
each with a glow and each floating gracefully out into the*

page. They were taking shape like the planets and stars of the universe.

Johnny laughed and clapped his hands, "Look, Daddy, look!" Stunned, Doug couldn't take his eyes off it.

"For the love of it," was printed on the page.

After a time, Doug turned to the next page and read, "The universe formed for the love of it."

"The birth of the universe feels like the birth of my son," Doug thought. "Incredible, indescribable joy."

Doug turned to the last page of the book.

It said, "Live life for the love of it."

What do you think it means to live life for the love of it?

How about:

- Fully engaging with life?
- Being fully present?
- Caring?
- Loving?
- Being passionate about what's important to you?
- Doing what you love?
- Being what you love?
- Being fully you?

Do you live life for the love of it?	
Ways in which you live life for the love of it.	Ways in which you don't live life for the love of it.

Are you afraid to live life for the love of it? You may not have had good experiences with fully engaging in life.

Perhaps you've had relationships that have gone wrong, or you haven't felt accepted in being fully you.

These kinds of experiences can cause you to close your heart because you've been hurt, and you limit who you are. When viewing the situation through a "physical world" lens, this looks like the safest approach. But what a high price to pay! Your fear is holding you hostage!

In actuality, being open-hearted — being fully you — is the safest and most fulfilling approach to life. This is because a closed heart leads to separation — from yourself and others.

Not being in full connection with yourself and others requires you to live life in a limited way. You make choices that are not the best for you, such as accepting a job or a relationship that doesn't fulfill you. Likewise, you can feel alone or afraid in this world because you're not in full connection.

Not being in full connection also means you miss joyful moments in life, as your full attention is not focused on the present.

Kristina Out of Connection

"What is happening?" Kristina exclaimed. "Every day it gets worse. I feel frantic and so alone in the world! What can I do to calm myself down?"

Then she remembered a meditation CD she'd purchased a couple weeks ago at a bookstore. After searching for a few minutes she found it. It felt at that moment like she'd discovered a gold mine. "I hope this helps!" she thought.

She got comfortable on her bed and switched on the CD player. The meditation began by having her focus on her breathing, then on relaxing her tense muscles. The soothing voice carried on from there…

Imagine you're on holiday in London, England. It's a beautiful day. The sun is shining pleasantly, and you're looking forward to what the time brings. You've been excited about this trip, as it feels full of potential. You've already spent a few days in England's green countryside, exploring some of the noblest of estates. It's been fun and interesting.

You're on this trip with Catherine, one of your best friends. She's spent a lot of time in England, and now that you're in London, she wants to take you to one of her favorite places, a museum. Actually, one particular part of a museum. It contains reproductions of some of the most celebrated Northern European and Spanish sculpture.

Catherine explains that plaster moulds were made from the original sculptures. This was often done in pieces, because the sculptures, particularly parts of buildings, were so large and intricate. The moulds were then used to create plaster reproductions of these architectural and other wonders. It sounds amazing to you!

So there you are.

You've had a scrumptious breakfast and are making your way to the museum, which is close by. It's a huge building — very roomy, with high ceilings and smooth marble walls.

Catherine leads you to the room devoted to the reproductions.

You step through the doorway and are immediately stunned by what lies before you. It's so stunning you can barely stay upright.

Catherine tells you she wants to go check out another part of the museum and will be back shortly. You barely hear her. The room has all of your attention. "All of these amazing creations are in one huge room!" you say to yourself. The astounding energy from each of these works of art is here, in this one place, and it feels like it is literally filling you.

It's as though every cell in your body is being fed!

You have not experienced this before, and you can't help but walk around. You want to see and feel all that is here. The first sculpture you encounter is the face of a building in Spain. It must be at least 50 feet high, and the patterns of circles and arches and geometric shapes are so compelling you can barely take your

eyes off them. So elegant, yet so powerful, that you feel your heart opening.

You read the placard by the sculpture. "Love is the most powerful energy of the universe. This work of art was sculpted with an open heart. Thus, hearts open in its presence."

Once again, you are stunned. You seek the solidness of a nearby bench, sit down, and take a look at the placard again. The reality of where you are, the museum, seems to be fading to another time. It feels as if you are there with the sculptor as he works on this masterpiece.

He is peaceful, his open heart infusing love into every action. You feel as he feels — full, complete, satisfied. "How could this be?" you think to yourself. "He has no fear, no worry, no doubt!"

Then understanding comes to you. Most of us live with closed hearts. We live this way because we think it is the safest approach to life, when in fact, the opposite is true.

A closed heart leads to separation — from love, from ourselves and from others. Not being in full connection allows us to take non-feeling actions such as physically or emotionally hurting ourselves or another, polluting the Earth, or valuing money over people. We could not possibly do these things if we lived with open hearts, in full connection to ourselves and all that is around us.

Opening our hearts allows full connection with ourselves, others, and the Earth. It allows full connection to love, the most powerful energy of the universe. Love is an energy so strong that fear and worry cannot exist in its presence.

You can feel your own fear and worry dissolving as your heart opens. It opens simply because you're in the presence of the sculptor. You can see that it's almost impossible to be around a truly open heart — around true love — without opening your own heart. You understand now that the more open hearts we have in this world, the better it is for all of us. Open hearts are the path to peace and joy.

Your eyes focus again on the placard by the sculpture: "Love is the most powerful energy of the universe. This work of art was sculpted with an open heart. Thus, hearts open in its presence."

You stand up from the bench with your opened heart and move to a sculpture that seems to be calling to you from the other side of the room. It's a very tall column with many images sculpted in a spiral rising all the way up to the top. "What is it about?" you wonder.

At the base of the column you see carvings of the surfaces of the Earth — mountains, streams, canyons and oceans.

Further up you see trees and flowers, rocks and desert sand. Next are insects and animals, then people. Higher up on the column you can see the sun and moon and clouds. And at the pinnacle, you can just make out what looks like the divine of the universe.

Having learned from the last time, you sit down at the nearby bench first and then look at the placard for the sculpture. It reads: "Full possibility lies within. During the sculpting of this pathway, the artist shifted her reference point from the Earth to the heavens, opening full possibility within her. Enter the pathway here."

You look around, but don't see any pathway. And then you feel it — movement. Movement through time.

You've gone back into the past again, only now you're with the sculptor of the column.

It is evening, and the sculptor is working feverishly on the bottom row of images of the surfaces of the Earth. With her is her mother — providing nourishment, understanding, and encouragement.

It is through her mother's heart that you understand all: the sculptor, a young woman, a physician just beginning in her new profession.

Such a gift she has for art, and an even greater gift for healing.

The medical knowledge she gained during her formal training has been essential; but the ways of thinking and being she learned during her studies feel limiting to this courageous young woman. Her feverish work on the sculpture is her attempt to open something — she's just not sure what.

Her mother understands that the medical training turned her daughter's eye to the physical world. Her daughter came to believe that what is possible in life is only what can be seen in the physical world. Her mother knows that this is a limited, inaccurate point of view. She encourages her daughter to rediscover the truth.

You watch the daughter, evening after evening, late into the night. She is sculpting her way up the column, spiral by spiral.

And as she progresses you notice that her manner becomes less feverish. Her heart becomes more open, and her gaze moves, spiral by spiral, from the Earth to the heavens.

By the time she reaches the top of the column, the spiral representing the divine of the universe, she is no longer limiting possibility to what she can see in the physical world.

She has shifted her reference point, spiral by spiral, to the heavens. She now understands, and so do you, that to allow full possibility, one must measure possibility by what is possible in the divine — seen or unseen — not by what only appears possible in the physical.

This is a tremendous relief to her, and to you, as you notice you are again focusing on the placard underneath the sculpture: "Full possibility lies within. During the sculpting of this pathway, the artist shifted her reference point from the Earth to the heavens, opening full possibility within."

You are reluctant to leave the museum.

There is much more to discover, yet you know it is time.

As you look back at the two sculptures one last time, you notice that the placards you had focused on are no longer there. Somehow, this doesn't surprise you. It opens the possibility that at any time, in any place, you might see a new placard and gain another amazing understanding. You can't wait!!

Live life fully — for the love of it, and for the love of you.

Love profoundly impacts everything it touches.

We know that children grow up healthier, happier, and more able to reach their full potential when they live in environments in which they are loved. The same is true for adults. This is because love and connection are the heart of our well-being.

Without the heart, we have nothing.

Ever talk with older people about their lives? If you do, then you know that they seldom say, "I wish I had worked more" or "I wish I had seen more movies." Almost without fail, older people will tell you they wish they had spent more quality time with their loved ones. They frequently say that their life of experience has helped them to understand what true priorities are, and they wish they had understood these priorities sooner.

The same sentiment is often echoed by those who have experienced or are experiencing life-threatening situations. They quickly see what is most important to them. It generally isn't the house or fast internet access or their work responsibilities. It *is* their loved ones.

Kristina in Connection

When the meditation CD finished, Kristina smiled. "I feel better," she thought. "I've been feeling frantic and alone because my heart was closed to connection. I had shut out all true connection." Encouraged, Kristina called her two cycling buddies and invited them to dinner. Next she headed outside to go to the store for dinner supplies. Her heart melted when she noticed the spring flowers blooming by the front gate. "How long have they been there?" she wondered.

Just then the little neighbor boy, Adam, ran right up to her and gave her a hug. It brought tears to her eyes.

"Wow," she thinks now. "I've been missing out!"

A squeeze, a wink, or an appropriate touch can make all the difference. When such gestures are given to you, they are an acknowledgement of you and of the fact that we are all in this together.

Did you know that even just watching someone connect with another person, or watching them do something special for someone else, has a positive effect on you? You feel it. It lifts your spirit.

Jeff's School Project

"Interesting," Mr. Messner said. "An interesting proposal for a project."

Jeff became worried. "What does interesting mean?" he wondered. He had talked it out with his dad last night, and his dad was usually a pretty good gauge of whether something would be approved...

Jeff was proposing to track the impact of smiles. He figured that smiling at someone, genuinely smiling at someone, made both him and the other person happier. Therefore, both would then be more likely to smile at others, passing on the happiness. Didn't that make sense?

Mr. Messner smiled at Jeff. "Let's give it a try," he said.

Jeff smiled back happily.

A smile is a gift we can give each other. It's free, it's easy, and it feels good! The opportunities to give away smiles are endless.

Make a true connection and its effects multiply across the planet for the good of all concerned.

Remember, it is impossible to over-estimate the power of love and connection. Love and connection are the heart of your well-being. Open your heart and you have everything. Live life for the love of it!

In the next chapter you'll learn how to better understand your life's circumstances by viewing them with more than your physical eye.

.

Chapter 2

Mistake #2—
Trying to Understand Life from a
"Physical World Perspective"

Have you ever experienced a series of difficulties — like maybe you lost your wallet, then your relationship broke up, and then you became ill?

Were you falling apart or falling together?

Sometimes it's hard to tell.

For example, if you have been laid off from work recently, it probably feels like you're falling apart. But if you look at the situation from a broader perspective — a more spiritual perspective — you may find that being laid off from work is actually part of falling together.

Perhaps that job wasn't taking you in the direction you needed to go for your own development, your self-actualization. Being laid off could motivate you to look in other directions for opportunities that are more beneficial to you in your development as a human being in this physical world.

Trying to understand and live life from only a physical-world perspective is much like trying to understand baseball by watching only the third baseman — your perspective isn't broad enough. Understand life's situations better by widening your view.

Let's look at some example situations and how they might be understood when looking at them through a physical-world lens, as compared to a lens that allows a broader, more spiritual view.

Gabriella's Job Loss

Gabriella was a dedicated manager who ran a profitable business unit in a large health care company.

One day the company announced they were merging her department with another, and she was out of a job.

"I'm so surprised about this," she said to herself. "Wasn't I doing good work? Maybe my boss sold me out!"

With no notice and only three months severance, she was angry and afraid. Her family depended on her income.

She began to apply for positions in other companies right away. It was an anxious time for her and her family, and Gabriella definitely felt like she was "falling apart."

However, after two months of looking, she began work at a medical insurance firm, managing an even larger department than before.

Now Gabriella understands she wasn't falling apart, she was "falling together." She's paid well, is learning a great deal, and loves her new co-workers. She is much happier in this new job than the old one — and she never would have found it if she hadn't been laid off.

Your physical-world thoughts about why you lost your job might be that you lost it simply because of bad luck, or because of a boss that didn't like you. Another physical-world view might be that you lost the job because you weren't good enough.

In contrast, the broader spiritual understanding of a lost job could be that you were let go because everything that needed to happen in that job did happen, so it was time to move on.

Another possible spiritual perspective is that you lost the job because it wasn't the right situation for you and your optimal growth. You lost it because you needed to be motivated to look elsewhere for a position that would be more helpful to you at that point in your life.

Why did you lose your job?	
Possible Physical World Perspectives	Possible Spiritual Perspectives
Bad luck Bad boss You're not good enough	What needed to happen in the job occurred; now it's time to move on The job was not the best situation for your optimal growth and development You needed to create room for a new job

John's Lost Wallet

John had just gotten home and was about to put his wallet in his bedroom drawer, when he noticed he didn't have it! He frantically looked in his truck, but it wasn't there either.

"When did I use it last? Oh! At the fast food restaurant!" He drove back right away, but to no avail — no wallet anywhere.

Panic started to set in. "What am I going to do?" he kept thinking. "No cash, no credit card, no ID. How am I even going to pay for lunch tomorrow?"

He went home, settled down a bit, and called the credit card company to cancel his card.

He then made a list of everything else that he could remember was in his wallet, so that he could begin the process of replacing it.

He realized there wasn't much he needed to replace — telephone numbers he didn't use anymore, a photo of his old girlfriend...

In thinking about the contents of his wallet, John realized he had been hanging on to the past without even noticing! He needed to let go of the past so that he could move forward.

Feeling positive about the future for the first time in a long while, he headed to his brother's to borrow some cash.

Your physical-world perspective on why you lost your wallet may be that you lost it because you're absent-minded and didn't keep track of it properly, or because you just have rotten luck and you're always losing things.

Looking at this situation from a broader spiritual perspective, perhaps you lost your wallet because it was time for a "new identity," or it was time for you to reconsider who you are.

Why did you lose your wallet?	
Possible Physical World Perspectives	Possible Spiritual Perspectives
Bad luck	It's time to reconsider who you are
You didn't keep track of it as you should have	It's time for a "new identity"
	It's time to let the past go and move forward

Tu's Illness

"What is the problem?" Tu thought. His balance wasn't right, and he couldn't seem to control his fingers well enough to play the classical guitar — his love for more than 30 years. He'd been having problems for months, and the doctors still didn't know the cause.

Becoming edgier with each day he couldn't play, Tu's edginess turned to desperation. Then one day in a frantic attempt to connect with the notes, he wrote a line of music. And then he wrote another, and another, and another. Exhilarating!

He discovered a whole new way of connecting! He couldn't believe it! Tu wasn't sure he would ever have experienced this if he hadn't been so desperate.

Using a physical-world lens, you might think you're sick simply because you're around germs. Or, you might think you have an illness because you're being punished by God for something you've done.

When you apply a broader, more spiritual understanding to the illness, you may find that coping with the illness requires you to see or experience things you might have missed otherwise.

Or you may be sick to motivate you to bring all of your energy to the here and now to overcome the illness, instead of losing your energy to other things such as worry or the past. It's also possible you have the illness because being sick will require you to receive help from others, and you need to learn how to receive.

Why are you ill?	
Possible Physical World Perspectives	**Possible Spiritual Perspectives**
You've been around too many germs	You need to be reminded to care properly for yourself
You haven't been getting enough rest	
You're being punished by God for something you've done	You need to slow down to see or experience things you might miss otherwise
	You need to learn to receive help from others
	You need to bring your energy to the here and now (not the past or the future)

Janet's Relationship Break Up

Janet and Derek had been married for 19 years when he told her he wanted a divorce. She couldn't believe her ears. "How did this happen?" she gasped.

In shock, she thought through the last number of years. "It's true," she realized. "We haven't really connected lately, particularly since the kids became teenagers. We've disagreed so much about how to handle their rebelliousness. With this on top of the long hours we've both been working, our marriage has certainly been strained."

Janet fell into a deep depression. She felt like a failure.

How could she carry on?

A co-worker told her about a support group for women going through divorce.

Out of pain and desperation, she tried it.

Through many months of talking with this small group of women, Janet began to understand more. She saw that her life had become stagnant. She had forgotten about growth, joy, and the wonders of breathing each breath.

Janet now feels that her divorce stunned her out of her stagnation. She sees many challenges ahead, but she is thankful for the wake-up call.

Looking through a physical-world lens, it might seem your relationship broke up because you weren't worthy of love, or you weren't good enough. Or perhaps you feel the opposite — that it was actually your intimate partner that wasn't good enough. Or that it was just a matter of bad luck.

Broadening your perspective to a spiritual view, you may find that what needed to happen in the relationship did happen, so it was simply time to move on. Or you may see from the spiritual point of view that this situation wasn't the best for you.

Why did your relationship break up?	
Possible Physical World Perspectives	**Possible Spiritual Perspectives**
Bad luck	What was to occur in the relationship did occur, meaning it was time to move on
Bad partner	
You weren't worthy of love	This wasn't the best situation for you
You weren't good enough	You needed to create room for a new relationship
	You needed motivation to develop and grow

Serge's Tsunami Experience

When Serge saw the news about the Asian Tsunami of 2004, it shook him to his core. Such a strong force that caused such tragedy, and there was nothing anyone could do to stop it.

"You can't prevent natural disasters like this!" he thought. "My life could change at any moment—I could lose all that's important to me!" Serge felt afraid in a way he hadn't experienced before.

As he watched the stories on the news in the days and weeks after the disaster, he saw people's tragic experiences. He saw that the safety of loved ones was the biggest thing on their minds.

He also noticed that people directly affected by the tsunami reconnected with the spiritual aspects of their lives as they sought comfort and understanding.

Watching this process of reconnecting helped Serge truly understand what is most important in life. It is with this new-found awareness that he now lives each day.

Your physical-world ideas about why natural disasters occur may range from "It is simply bad luck," to "God is unhappy with us," to "The world must be coming to an end."

If you looked at these disasters from a broader, more spiritual view, you might see that such experiences remind people of what the true priorities are in life. You might also see that natural disasters motivate people to stop gazing so steadily at the ground and start looking upward, to reconnect with spirit and the higher realms of understanding.

Why do we experience natural disasters?	
Possible Physical World Perspectives	**Possible Spiritual Perspectives**
Bad luck God is unhappy The world is coming to an end	They help us look to the spiritual for comfort and understanding of what occurred — reconnecting us to spirit and the higher realms of life They help us to get clear about true priorities They highlight the importance of love and connection

There is more to life than meets the eye —the physical eye, that is.

Your life circumstances can be viewed by more than your physical eye. Seeing your life through a broader spiritual lens will make more sense than viewing it through a physical-world lens.

This broader view is your "spiritual home field advantage," and applies to all of your experiences — whether you have a broken computer, parenting problems, or feelings of anxiety.

Think of your physical life as a field trip. Most of your existence — your eons and eons of existence — is lived at "Home" in the spiritual realm. You have physical lives — field trips — so that you can learn and contribute in specific ways. Thus, when things happen in your physical life, like the loss of a job, they happen for a reason.

Everything happens for a purpose. Losing your job may be what you need in order to be pointed in a different direction — a direction that will help you and all concerned achieve everything that you came here to achieve.

Remember, there's generally more to the story than meets the eye... the physical eye, that is. So turn that eye to the broader perspective of the spiritual realm to understand what life's situations are really about.

The good news is that you're not in this alone — it is not a solo journey. Read on for more information about the help you have around you.

Chapter 3

Mistake #3 —
Thinking Life Is a Solo Journey

Do you feel that when it comes down to it, you're alone in the world?

Do you wonder if anyone is here for you? Have you wondered if you can only count on yourself?

Actually, nothing could be further from the truth.

At "Home" in the spiritual realm, you have a large family of loved ones — your spirit or soul family.

Some of these loved ones come with you on your field trips to Earth. Perhaps you've had the experience of feeling a strong connection to someone you just met… It's probably because you know them from "Home."

Yessenia Meets Gloria

Driving to work one morning, Yessenia turned the corner on a street near her house and heard the pop of a tire. She knew immediately what it was and pulled over to the side of the road.

Her persistent father had taught her how to change a tire when she was in high school. But the thought of having to haul out the spare tire and tools, jack up the car, wrestle with the flat tire — and get her clothes dirty, to boot — deflated her, just like the tire she needed to change.

While rummaging around her trunk for the jack, a truck pulled up behind her. Out jumped Gloria with a big smile on her face. Beside her was her husband, Juan.

Juan stepped in and took over the tire change, while Gloria introduced herself.

She then told Yessenia about a funny experience she recently had with a flat tire.

Yessenia felt as if they had known each other all their lives. And indeed, their friendship has become one of her most treasured relationships.

Most of us like to have company on these physical journeys, these field trips to Earth. Otherwise it could be a pretty lonely experience.

You may run into your family members from "Home" at any time on your physical journey here. Your history together often makes it easy to step right into a friendship with them.

It gets even better, though. Some of your loved ones who don't come with you on your Earth field trips volunteer to help you while you're here.

Everyone in the spirit realm knows how challenging it can be in this physical world, so you're sent here with angels, guides and teachers who can see the whole picture for your life.

They have the spiritual home field advantage, and share it with you.

Your angels and guides help you navigate this physical realm so that you can achieve all that you set forth to achieve. They nudge you in various ways when you need to do something differently.

Nudges Mike Received From His Guides

First as a grocery store stocker, then checker, and then manager, Mike was quite successful in his job. It took five years to move up the ladder, and he was proud of what he had accomplished.

However, the store had recently been taken over by a new owner, and Mike wasn't finding it as easy to work for him. Mike got the sense that it might have been time to look for a different job.

"Perhaps it could be with a larger chain of stores," he considered. "That would allow me to continue to move up the ranks."

Still fairly comfortable with his job, though, he decided to stay with it for a while longer.

Then the new owner took charge of the hiring of new staff for the store, a responsibility that had been Mike's. Unfortunately, the staff hired by his new boss didn't seem to have the same commitment to the job as previous staff.

"It's getting harder and harder to maintain the quality of service in the store," Mike thought. "These new people aren't staying with the job as long, so I'm training new people all the time."

Again, Mike sensed that it was time to look for a new job, but he couldn't seem to get himself motivated to get out there and see what was available. "It's all so much work!" he said to himself. "And besides, it'll probably settle down here."

Unfortunately for Mike, the situation with the new owner continued to deteriorate. At each turn, Mike had an even stronger sense that the time was right to look for a new job, but he didn't follow this sense and was eventually laid off.

⌐◡⌐

Those senses that he should look for a new job were all opportunities — nudges from Mike's spirit guides — to make a change that was needed for his well-being. This might have been a new job or some other circumstance that would have been better for him.

However, Mike didn't act on these nudges, so eventually he wasn't given a choice.

Remember that from your limited physical-world view, your view of third base, it may look as though Mike's layoff was a problem for him.

However, you need to consider the entire ball game. You need to view the situation from the broader perspective of the spiritual realm so that you can understand the layoff was really a way to connect Mike with something better — a way to motivate him to look for something better.

Changes, such as a job layoff, create space for new things to occur.

⌐◡⌐

Vanessa's Running Away

Vanessa was unhappy. Something was eating away at her. She was short-tempered with her husband and children.

She wanted independence, so she left the house more and more. She spent a lot of time with her girlfriends and at the gym on a new intensive exercise program.

Her relationships with her husband and children deteriorated. But it felt almost as though she had a fever. The more she was away, the more she wanted to be away.

Somewhere deep inside she knew she was running away from something, but she couldn't seem to make herself stop and face it.

Then one day during her exercise routine she injured her leg so badly that she required surgery and significant recuperation time.

"Now I can't leave!" Vanessa worried.

"What am I going to do? It'll be a month or more before I can even hobble around!"

The injury has left Vanessa with little choice but to work through what has been haunting her.

In the process, she is rediscovering her family and all that she loves about them.

She is rediscovering herself.

Just like Mike, Vanessa received nudges from her guides to handle her situation in a better way. The ultimate nudge was the injury that made it impossible for her to continue running and required her to come to terms with what was bothering her.

Your spirit guides and teachers truly guide and teach. They know what you came to achieve during this physical incarnation.

This bigger-picture knowledge allows them to nudge you in directions that will be most fulfilling for you. Spirit guides "help" you with actions like a lost job because of their care and concern for you and what you set out to do in this life. They want you to succeed, and something like a job loss may simply be a course correction.

You've probably noticed that when one door closes, another opens.

Your task is to pay attention. Notice when a door is closing, then look around to find where another door is opening. Look all around for that open door, as it often pops up in unexpected places.

Communication with Your Guides and Teachers

We all communicate with our guides and teachers, though for many of us, the process of receiving information from them isn't totally conscious. You may have gut feelings, intuition, or just a "knowing" about what to do.

This is your guidance stepping in and helping out, providing you with your spiritual home field advantage.

Unfortunately, like many of us, you may have the dreadful habit of ignoring the senses you get about what you need to be doing.

Do you ignore the senses you get about what you need to do?	
Examples of messages you may receive about what you need to do for your well-being	Possible consequences if you ignore the messages about what you need to do
Exercise Eat healthy food Meditate	Won't have the energy or good physical health to fully enjoy life, participate in an upcoming opportunity, or complete what you came to this physical world to do
Listen more, talk less	Miss out on critical information Miss the opportunity to form balanced connections with people
Apologize Forgive	Leave unfinished business Hold yourself back from possible growth and joy Miss an opportunity for an honest exchange with someone
Go to a class or training	Miss out on critical information Get caught without the knowledge or skills needed for an upcoming opportunity
Reach out to someone	Lose out on an experience that is intended to be of service to you and another person
Try something new	Miss out on an opportunity presented for your well-being
Slow down	Fail to see important opportunities because you're moving too fast Find yourself unable to fully enjoy what life has to offer

Senses of what you need to do for your well-being are messages from your spirit guides and teachers. These messages often start fairly low-key, but become stronger and stronger the longer you ignore them, until it's very difficult for you to continue to ignore them.

Over time, messages can become crystal clear. You've probably learned from experience that it pays to simply respond to your sense about what you need to do the first time around, instead of waiting until the opportunity is lost or the situation takes a turn for the worse.

Dominique's Heart Attack

Dominique didn't like to go to the doctor, so his annual physical had become more like his "every-5-year-physical."

Dominique viewed himself as a well-educated fellow who knew what he needed to do to stay healthy. "So why go see a doctor?" he thought.

He knew he needed to get enough rest, eat reasonably, and exercise. He knew he needed to do these things; he just generally didn't do them.

And although Dominique had recently noticed a decline in his energy level, he simply added an afternoon cup of coffee to his daily routine to try to make up for it.

Then one day when he was out shopping, he had a heart attack. "I can't believe I felt fine one minute, then the next minute I was being rushed to the hospital!" he told his friends. "Fortunately, the heart attack wasn't severe, but it certainly got my attention!"

Now he understands that staying healthy — getting enough rest, eating reasonably, and exercising — isn't optional.

Your guides and angels communicate with you, and you communicate with them.

You may do this in internal conversation (conversations you have in your head, seemingly with yourself,) questions, or requests.

This type of communication doesn't replace prayer, it augments it. Prayer is the most powerful form of communication with the divine.

Pray from your heart. Express your thanks. Express your love.

Pray for yourself. Pray for others. Pray for all.

As your guides and teachers communicate with you, you'll find that sometimes the messages make sense to you, such as, "It would be good to exercise more," or, "Relax, everything is fine," or, "Surprise her with a present," and "Tell him you're sorry."

And sometimes you may receive messages that aren't so straightfor-ward, such as, "It's time to find a new job."

With messages like this that feel more complicated, there's a certain amount of faith required to do as guided — faith in yourself and faith in something larger than you.

Angela's Diary Entries

Angela had always been a journal writer. Writing allowed her to see herself on the page before her, which helped her work through the many experiences of life.

The following is a particularly powerful set of feelings she experienced when her long-term relationship ended.

October 3 — Alone and Abandoned

I've been brought to my knees again. How often in life does this need to happen? How many broken hearts does one person, in one life, need to endure? How many times do I have to feel abandoned?

The answer that keeps appearing in my head is, "Until you understand that you're not alone and cannot be abandoned." Of course, why didn't I think of that? Continually experience circumstances in which I feel alone and abandoned so that I can learn I'm not alone or abandoned. Great — just the answer I was hoping for. I'm afraid of being alone, and because of this fear, there have been times when I've compromised myself — who I am — in order to keep from experiencing the feeling of being alone and an outsider in the world. I sold myself out. I let the fear take charge. I can't do that again.

October 5 — A Request

During my jog on the beach today I had my usual conversation with myself, only this time about belonging. I really need to get this thing about belonging. I really need to understand that I'm not alone and that I do belong. Please help me in learning this.

October 8 — The Twist of the Ankle

I was running across the street yesterday and hit a hole. I knew instantly when I heard the "pop" what it was all about. It was about learning "belonging". I don't know how this is going to help me learn, but somehow it is!

November 17 — An Understanding of Belonging

It's been five weeks and two days since I sprained my ankle. So what's been happening over the past 5 weeks? The expected restricted physical activity. None of the usual socializing at the gym. No morning jogs or walks in the valley. No going to the library, or bookstore, or even across the street to the cafe at work.

For some reason I've intuitively understood that I literally needed to "sit" with this in order to get it. No problem, since sitting and hobbling are about all I can do. I've spent a lot of time at the office. I've spent a lot of time at home alone. And quite frankly, I'm not sure exactly how it happened, but on Thursday, I realized a profound shift had occurred in my way of being in this world. Then on Friday, I was jogging again — slowly and carefully, with a taped ankle — but actually jogging!

The shift is simple, actually. It's a shift from an external orientation to an internal orientation. I've had a life of taking my cues about how to be in the world from the world — my not-so-welcoming family, co-workers, friends. It's been external input, screened by my internal set of values.

What's more, I used external input for balance. I sought out people and experiences to help balance me — to shore me up internally so that I wouldn't feel like an outsider, so that I wouldn't feel alone.

Now, miraculously, the external balancing no longer feels like a critical aspect of being. My balance and my understanding of belonging are now primarily internal. I can be who I am, without fear of being alone, because my foundation is now internal.

The internal is my connection to the spiritual, the larger aspects of life. From this vantage point I know I am not alone. I know I belong! Wow, this is such a tremendously calming change!

∽

Remember, you are not alone — you never have been, and you never will be. Your loved ones are with you whether you, or they, are in physical form or spirit form. They are with you forever and they are with you always.

Having guides and teachers helps you understand that your experience in life is not simply a matter of chance. Read on to learn more about your spiritual home field advantage and how your life circumstances and opportunities come about.

Chapter 4

Mistake #4 —
Thinking That Much of What Happens in Life is a Matter of Chance

Did you ever win something and figure it was just a lucky day?

Do you know people who seem to always be "lucky?"

Do you think that what happens in your life is the result of chance or luck?

The truth is there is no chance that life is left to chance.

Virtually every circumstance you encounter in this physical life is an opportunity to learn what you came here to learn, and to contribute what you came here to contribute.

Before you were born into this world, you determined what it was you wanted to achieve while you were here. You then worked with your advisors in the spiritual realm to develop circumstances in this physical life that would allow for the opportunities you needed to achieve these things.

When life appears to throw you a curve ball, it may actually be an opportunity to accomplish something on your physical life's "to do" list.

~

David's Mismatch

David felt that he was the oddball in his family. They were all athletic, regularly participating in sports like volleyball and bowling. They were extroverts who enjoyed social gatherings and hosting events at their home.

David's father was an avid football fan who dreamed of his son playing for his alma mater. He had even saved his old football jersey, and was proud it still fit him!

Introverted and introspective, David shied away from social gatherings and sports. He often took long walks in the hills surrounding his family's home so that he could have time to himself.

Nature comforted and fascinated him. He learned all he could about the foliage and animals and soil. He even took up environmental studies in college and eventually became a significant contributor in this field of science.

David's obvious mismatch with his family led him outside of his family circle, outside in nature, to discover a love of the environment.

This discovery gave him a heartfelt career and an opportunity to further humanity's knowledge and understanding of the environment.

Being a "misfit" in his family has also helped him to learn that being different doesn't mean "being less than." It simply means being different — of equal value and equally a part of the universe.

On David's physical-world "to do" list was to learn that he has equal worth even though he's different. In order to accomplish this learning, he set up the circumstance in which he was different from the rest of his family.

You, too, set up circumstances for your life so that you can complete your "to do" list. This "to do" list is a combination of things you came to learn and things you came to contribute.

Looking Through a Spiritual Lens, This is How it Works

Before you were born into this physical body, you set up a chart or map for yourself. It has a starting point and an ending point. The ending point is where you hope to be in your learning and development by the end of this physical life.

Your journey has many possible routes. The beautiful terrain can be rough and rocky or smooth as sand, depending on the choices you make. No matter which paths you choose, you have opportunities to achieve all that you came here to achieve.

If you pass up one opportunity, or even two, there will always be more. Virtually every circumstance you encounter is an opportunity. Take Yolanda for example…

Yolanda's Puppy

Yolanda was having a difficult time. In her mind, it had always been this way — she reasoned that she had a hard edge because life had a hard edge.

She had a good enough job, but she didn't enjoy it much — because of the people, mostly. She just didn't seem to get on with them very well. Not to mention that her boyfriend had recently broken up with her and her best friend moved to England with her new husband.

The one thing she did have was a puppy — left by her best friend, who couldn't take him to England with her.

Every day after work it was just her and the puppy. He was sickly, though. "He's so pitiful!" Yolanda thought.

She couldn't help but soften towards him. He made her laugh, the way he tried so hard to stay awake and play and then would just plop over asleep, often in her arms.

The days turned into weeks. Yolanda and the puppy became best buddies, and somehow that hard edge that Yolanda usually led with melted away.

Without even noticing it, she began to enjoy her job more, because people started to enjoy her more.

Yolanda has softened, and now life seems softer, too.

Being on her own with a sickly puppy was an opportunity for Yolanda to soften and enjoy life more.

Some opportunities to fulfill our physical-world "to do" list are easier than others. Yolanda could have passed up this particular opportunity to soften and live life in a different way.

Her next opportunity to experience this softening might then have been a stronger, more difficult circumstance — perhaps one so strong that it would have been hard to avoid the learning.

Look at Mark's situation below.

Mark's Illness

Mark loved his job. He was a construction contractor and worked on projects in various parts of the United States.

He had always been a strong man who enjoyed the physical activity of the job.

Unfortunately, Mark came down with an illness that made even normal physical activity feel strenuous.

For the first time in his adult life, he wasn't the physically strong person he had always been.

His standard way of approaching life — pushing his way through it — was no longer possible.

Since he got sick, Mark's illness has required him to approach life differently. He can't push his way through anymore.

Although it hasn't been easy, he is adjusting.

Working with people in his office each day, he is learning the arts of cooperation and negotiation.

He sees that he's much more successful with these approaches than he was with his old "pushing" style.

"Even better," he says to himself, "I have a girlfriend now. I guess there are advantages to being in one place for a while!"

For Mark, an illness that required him to change his way of life was like turning the volume up on a message he needed to hear.

Grace's Boss

"I want a different job!" Grace thought. She had only been in her current one for two months, but she could see she'd made a big mistake. Her boss had serious people issues,

clearly evident by his constant belittling of the staff and frequent yelling.

After the first time she saw him yell, Grace walked right into her boss's office and told him it wasn't right to treat people that way.

He took her statement as a declaration of war and stepped up his efforts to make her feel unwelcome.

Struggling with her own self-esteem, Grace worked to keep herself in balance. Even so, she found each interaction with her boss debilitating.

She did everything she could to find a new job, but nothing came through.

"This is so devastating!" Grace thought. "It feels like there's some kind of moratorium on new jobs. What am I going to do?"

Almost a year later, and a couple of months into a new job, Grace finally understood what that situation was about.

Her experience with that crazy boss had required her to strengthen inside.

She needed to stay in that job until her boss's behavior didn't negatively affect her self-esteem, until she could experience her boss's behavior for what it was — the immaturity of a person with serious problems.

The year-long nightmare served a good purpose for Grace, a purpose that will aid her for the rest of her life.

External Circumstances Are Opportunities!		
Circumstance In Your Life	What It Motivates You To Do	Possible Opportunities Being Provided
You feel different from the others in your family. You don't "fit" well with them.	Seek outside your family for a better fit. Consider them your "family of origin" and develop a "family of choice," made up of good friends.	To learn that being different is OK. To discover wonderful things about yourself and the world around you. To develop strong relationships outside of your family.
You are not well-loved or cared-for in your family.	Seek outside your family for a life in which you are well-loved and cared for. Develop a "family of choice."	To learn to love and care for yourself. To develop strong relationships outside of your family.
The traffic or weather is slowing you down, making you late.	Think through what's big and what's small in life — traffic is small, weather is small.	To learn how to handle everyday pressures well — to take them in stride. To develop trust that you'll get where you need to go when you need to be there. To have a few more minutes to relax in the car or prepare for your destination.

External Circumstances Are Opportunities!		
Circumstance In Your Life	**What It Motivates You To Do**	**Possible Opportunities Being Provided**
You do not get the job you wanted. You do not get accepted into the school you wanted.	Seek a different job. Seek a different school. Try again at a later date.	To realize that this job or school is not right for you, or the timing is not right. To get a different job or get into a different school that will take you in a better direction for your life, helping you to achieve what you came here to do. To get the job or get into the school at a time that is better for you. You may not be ready yet, or you have something else you need to do first.
A store does not have the product you want.	Look for a different product. Go to a different store. Try shopping online. Decide you don't need the product.	To find a different product, or a store that you like better. To learn a new skill. To discover you don't need the product.

External Circumstances Are Opportunities!		
Circumstance In Your Life	**What It Motivates You To Do**	**Possible Opportunities Being Provided**
You get sick.	Look for ways to become healthy. Change behavior so you can get healthy. Rest more. Slow down. Figure out how to live a good-quality life even with the illness.	To discover new things about yourself and the world around you. To change your life for the better. To develop strengths in new areas. To develop compassion.

Use this space to fill in your own experiences.		
Circumstance In Your Life	**What It Motivated You To Do**	**Possible Opportunity That Was Provided**

Some aspects of our lives are planned, such as possible opportunities to learn and contribute. At the same time, we have free will — we make choices about how we lead our lives.

Our job is to step up to the plate and take responsibility for how we lead our lives.

It's easy to think, "I just have bad luck," or, "No one will give me a break," or, "They hurt me, so that means I can hurt you." When you think these things, it's an avoidance of responsibility. You are responsible for how you handle yourself and your life, no matter what the external circumstance.

By the way, no one ever chooses circumstances in which they will be abused. Abuse occurs because abusers abuse — they exercise their free will in a negative way by hurting others.

Abuse is not acceptable in any way, in any situation.

Some people have more challenges than others at certain points in their lives, and some seem to handle them better than others.

Is that because of a willingness to step up to the plate and live life in the best way possible? Or is it because they understand what's really important in life — what the priorities are? Or both?

Jodie's Life

Jodie's diabetes began in childhood. As a middle-aged woman, she also suffered from kidney failure. Her husband was a wonderful man who she described as a blessing. They loved each other, and he stood with her no matter the medical issues. Their one child, Jessie, went with her mom to her dialysis appointments to keep her company. Jodie described her daughter the same way as her husband — "a blessing."

During her adult years Jodie lost her eyesight because of the diabetes. Amazingly, you never heard a complaint from her. She met people with a smile.

The staff at the dialysis unit became her friends. More blessings in her life — and theirs as well.

Recently Jodie's husband died from a massive heart attack.

Alone with their early-teenage daughter, Jodie is now adapting. Giving up is not a part of who she is.

She remains positive — a true teacher for those around her.

Even though Jodie has significant issues to cope with, she appreciates the many good things around her — love, life, people, and relationships. Her positive attitude and understanding of what's truly important in life are significant contributions. She leads by example.

Lighten Up

Another critical element in this journey of life is a lightness of spirit, an ability to keep from taking everything so heavily, so seriously.

Have you been around people who seem to see the funny side of almost everything?

They lighten the mood, and brighten the room, just by their ability to see things from a different vantage point.

George and His Son

George struggled with a son much like David (whose story appeared at the beginning of this chapter.) George had plans for his son — things he had thought about even before Andy was born. He too had played football in college and dreamed about the day he could teach the game to Andy. Maybe his son would even become a star!

But Andy just didn't seem interested. Other nine-year-olds played on teams, but George's son wouldn't even throw the ball back and forth in the yard.

George was a good man and a good father, but he felt he had been cheated. "Am I being punished?" he had wondered. "It's so aggravating! I love football so much. How could I have a son who doesn't?"

Then one day the family was watching one of George's daughters play in her softball league championship. Everyone was engrossed in the game but Andy. He was fascinated with some bugs he'd found. He kept picking them up and trying to put them on the picnic blanket, but they'd scurry away.

But Andy was not deterred! He kept at it, laughing all the while.

George could see how much fun his son was having and in an instant realized that he needed to follow Andy's example. He needed to lighten up and enjoy his son for who he was.

Now when George thinks about Andy he can't help but smile! What a big lesson he learned from his son!

Not taking things so heavily — seeing the lighter side — can really help you as you move through life. Develop your sense of humor and you'll be able to see the many lighter, and often amusing, sides of life's many happenings!

Step Up

Our job is to "step up to the plate" and take responsibility for how we lead our lives. We're not left alone, though, to wander the world by ourselves.

As described in the last chapter, your spirit guides and teachers help you navigate this physical world. They help you make good choices and take advantage of the opportunities you're presented — so that you might accomplish all that is possible.

You may have a gut feeling, an intuition, or just a "knowing" about what to do as you make your way through each day. This is your guidance stepping in and helping out, helping you connect with your spiritual home field advantage. Everyone around you is invested in your success, because they want you to be successful as an individual, and because every bit of learning and development that any one of us achieves helps us all.

The next chapter explains how we're all connected. It shows how important your life is for you — as well as for the entire universe — and how your progress is everyone's progress.

Remember, there is no chance that life is left to chance. Some of it is planned and some of it is left up to your free will. Use the help of guidance to effectively navigate the physical world so that you might achieve all that you came to achieve.

Chapter 5

Mistake #5 —
Thinking That You and Your Life
Are Not of Consequence

Do you wonder about the point of it all? If your life has any consequence? If all of this pain and difficulty is worth it?

Have you ever heard the song that goes, "You are everything, and everything is you?" In the larger scheme of things, you *are* everything and everything *is* you. **There's no such thing as a small, inconsequential life, because we're all connected. Each life is of tremendous consequence to the individual and to all of existence.**

How are we all connected?

Energy is the core of it. Everything is made of energy. A chair, for example, is simply energy in a form that's more dense or consolidated than other forms of energy, such as air or light.

Human beings are made of energy. You are your own discrete drop of energy, like a drop of water in the ocean.

All drops of energy are connected, just as all drops of water in the ocean are connected. And just as every drop of water *is* the ocean, you are also the ocean. You are a drop of energy in the ocean of energy, and you are all energy itself.

So what does this mean in your daily life?

Every thought you have and every action you take impacts everything else — everything that exists.

Every bit of your learning and development makes it easier for others to learn and develop.

Each act of kindness, each act of love, has an impact. It helps you and everyone else in the quest to learn, contribute, and evolve.

Rosa's Way

Rosa, the new head waitress at Café Phoenix, wondered what the other staff had experienced before she was hired. "They're all so jumpy and afraid," she thought. "What happened?"

One of the waitresses, Terry, finally confided in her. "The last head waitress watched us like a hawk, swooping down on us at every turn. It was like she expected we wouldn't do our jobs!"

Appalled, Rosa became even more conscious of treating the waitresses with respect. She coached them when needed, but in a way that helped them feel good about themselves and improve their skills.

Rosa has had a positive effect on the entire staff at the Café. It has taken time — more than a year of building relationships and helping staff to feel their value. Waitresses and cooks alike smile now. Their lives at work are good. Even better, they've experienced Rosa's way of trust and respect, and it has changed them. They feel better inside — about themselves and the world.

Like Rosa, you have a purpose in being here. Each one of us does. There are the visible examples, like the famous missionary Mother Teresa, and there are the not-so-visible examples, like Rosa.

You have a critical role to play. Sometimes it's hard to know what that role is, because often you can only see one part of the picture, like third base. If you could see the whole picture, the whole ball game — if you could see life through a spiritual lens — you could better understand your critical role in the action. What may appear to you to be inconsequential may actually be of great significance.

Alone Again

Estranged from his biological family, Devon felt even more alone since he'd broken up with his partner. And on top of his relationship troubles, work was more stressful than ever. The daily routine of fighting the traffic, spending long days in his cubicle answering the telephone, then going home tired and frustrated was overwhelming. "What's the point?" he wondered.

Mike worked in a different department than Devon, but had run into him in the employee lounge a couple of times. He would have liked to get to know Devon, but felt he didn't have the time to strike up much of a conversation. On this particular Friday, however, Mike made a point to stop by Devon's desk.

They spoke amicably and discovered they were actually from the same town and knew some of the same people. They also shared a similar hobby — genealogy.

When Devon left the office that night, he felt lighter. He felt hopeful. On his way home he even stopped at his favorite book store to participate in a discussion group about a book he'd recently read. He hadn't done that in a long time. It felt good.

Mike may never know the difference he made for Devon by simply stopping by his desk. Looking through your physical eyes, you just can't see most of the impact of your actions.

Sophie's Move

Sophie was excited about her recent move to Beijing and her first international assignment with her company. Happy about the professional opportunity, she gladly accepted the challenge, even though she didn't know a single person in China.

This aspect of the move — building a life in addition to work — felt daunting to her. "I'm so shy when it comes to socializing," she thought. "What can I do?"

One day she saw an advertisement for a women's coffee sponsored by an expatriate organization. She made herself go. She knew she would never meet anyone if she didn't get out of her apartment!

She entered the large hall and almost froze in her tracks when she saw what looked like a sea of women. They all seemed to know each other. Everyone had someone to sit with. She wanted to flee from the room.

Instead, she took a deep breath and wove her way through the tables to find an empty seat. "Hi, I'm Sophie and I just moved to Beijing last week," was all she needed to say.

The women around the table gave her warm smiles. They welcomed her and started talking and laughing about their experiences with arriving in Beijing.

Before she knew it, Sophie had several dinner invitations, and now she has much useful information about how to adapt in this new country. These days she can't help smiling.

This group of women made all the difference for Sophie. They didn't know when they woke up that morning that they would make such a difference for someone. Something you can be sure of, though, is that they — and you — are of consequence each and every day.

Do you give away smiles that are contagious? Do people feel better just by being around you? Then your life is of consequence. Your smile can give another person hope. Likewise, a touch or a hug can be huge to someone who is feeling unlovable.

Your Contributions	
Ways to Contribute	Possible Impacts of Your Contributions
Appreciate, be grateful, be thankful, say thank you Appreciate differences	Help others understand their value Help you understand the value of the people and things around you
Smile, laugh, enjoy, have fun	Lighten and brighten the moment Bring joyful energy to the world Help you and those around you feel happier Help keep you and those around you balanced Boost your health
Learn	Allow advancement that may not otherwise occur Provide an atmosphere of growth for others Provide opportunities for growth by sharing what you have learned Keep you interested and engaged

Your Contributions	
Ways to Contribute	**Possible Impacts of Your Contributions**
Listen	Allow advancement that may not otherwise occur
	Help people feel valued
	Help you to develop compassion
	Help others understand that listening is an important part of connection
	Provide opportunities for growth
	Keep you interested and engaged
Have courage	Develop strength in you and others
Have integrity	Increase self-esteem and confidence for you and others
	Allow advancement that may not otherwise occur
	Help others to have courage and integrity
Respect others and the Earth	Support others in being themselves
	Support others in reaching their full potential
	Help others understand their value
	Help others develop respect for themselves
	Allow respect for you
	Help keep the Earth healthy

Your Contributions	
Ways to Contribute	**Possible Impacts of Your Contributions**
Connect with others and the Earth	Allow you and others to feel a part of each other — not alone

Allow you and others to understand each other

Allow you and others to understand your mutual value

Allow you to feel a part of the Earth

Allow you to value the Earth |
| Be your best

Be genuine

Be creative | Help you to contribute fully to others and the world

Encourage others to do the same

Allow advancement that may not otherwise occur

Help others feel good themselves

Help you stay connected with yourself

Help you to feel good about yourself |
| Love and forgive — yourself and others

Care — about needs, events, daily happenings

Hug, give loving touches | Help those you love and care about to flourish

Help you flourish

Connect you to others and others to you

Connect you to the world

Keep you interested and engaged |

Your Contributions	
Ways to Contribute	**Possible Impacts of Your Contributions**
Lend strength, provide support, cheer someone on Have compassion Be generous	Help you and others reach full potential Connect you to others and others to you Help you feel good about yourself and others
Pray, have a spiritual practice	Help you to reach your full potential Help you contribute fully to others and the world Support your healing Allow learning and advancement that may not otherwise occur
Share ideas Voice problems Solve problems	Support connection to others Help others feel included and connected to you Bring important issues to the surface so they can receive attention Allow learning that may not otherwise occur Keep you interested and engaged
Have patience	Allow the full situation to unravel Allow greater understanding Keep your stress level down

Your Contributions	
Ways to Contribute	**Possible Impacts of Your Contributions**
Lead, participate, motivate

Share a skill | Allow action or change that may not otherwise occur

Provide support for others

Provide opportunities for learning and advancement for you and others |

Use this space to fill in your own contributions.	
Ways to Contribute	**Possible Impacts of Your Contributions**

These are only some of the ways you can and do have consequence in this world. Our lives are interrelated, like drops of water in the ocean.

We're each here for our own journey, as well as the journeys of others. We're all in this together!

How have others made a difference for you?

Joseph's Loss

Joseph lost his wife to a sudden death. Afterwards it seemed that almost everywhere he went he met someone who talked about a recent major loss they had experienced.

This happened whether he was waiting at the doctor's office, or on a flight to a business meeting, or at the gym. Total strangers opened right up to him with no prompting on his part.

Joseph was able to listen, share his own experience with loss, and offer some tools he used during the most difficult parts of the grief process.

People seemed to be drawn to him for guidance.

It has been a long road, but Joseph is now at peace with his wife's passing.

Through his journey of pain and coming to peace, he has been able to connect with others in an entirely new way that feels rewarding and comforting to him.

Joseph's personal grief brought him new understandings. His significant loss helped him grow, and helped him connect with and provide assistance to others.

You, too, may not be the headline sports player, actor, or recording artist. However, your consequence in this world cannot be measured by headlines.

~⌒~

Water Boy Needed

"The team needs a water boy. Are there any volunteers?"

The group of teenagers kept their eyes to the ground, avoiding the coach's gaze. Water Boy was a loser job.

Miles approached the coach later and quietly volunteered for the job. He really wanted to play soccer, but he knew he wasn't a strong player.

He figured he would be of more help to the team by making sure there was plenty of water on those hot summer practice days.

Besides, he'd also have a great view of the games from directly on the sideline.

The team made it to the championship. Everyone got to go to the final, including the water boy. On the sideline, Miles' constant good cheer helped keep the spirit of the team up.

He rooted for them, patted them on the back, and encouraged them when they were disappointed in their play.

Then it happened. A tie at the end of regulation, no score during overtime, and penalty kicks to decide it all. And the goal that won the game!

Miles was just as happy as the players. And he'd had a great time! The boys were jubilant and celebratory — lots of hugging and shouting.

When the players went off to the locker room, Miles was left alone to clean up. As he put the water coolers on the carts, he grinned from ear to ear.

When Miles thinks back on the big game, he knows what a difference he made.

Remember, your life is of tremendous consequence to you and to others because we're all connected. Every thought you have and every action you take impacts everything else — everything that exists.

Every bit of your learning and development makes it easier for others to learn and develop.

Each act of kindness, each act of love, helps you and everyone else in the quest to learn, contribute, and evolve. Like the song says, you are everything, and everything is you.

Miles made a difference. You make a difference.

Life isn't all about giving, however. Receiving is just as important, as you'll read in the next chapter.

Chapter 6

Mistake #6 —
Living Life as Though it is All About Receiving or as Though it is All About Giving

Is it easier for you to give than to receive? Or is it easier to receive than to give?

Do you wonder why some people "receive" more money, or happiness, or friends in their lives, than you do?

Is giving more important — more spiritual — than receiving?

Giving and receiving are equally important. But let's be clear. Receiving doesn't mean taking and giving doesn't mean sacrificing.

$\backsim$

To Receive

At age 38, Joan's arthritis was so bad she couldn't take care of some of the basic chores around the house.

Nor could she provide all that the kids required, especially since being the chauffeur to basketball, cheerleading, and band had become such a large part of her parental role.

Driving was impossible some days, because the arthritis prevented her from even grasping the steering wheel!

Joan became more and more distraught as the arthritis worsened. "I've always been so strong," she thought. "I've never needed help like this before. I can't stand that I need so much assistance, but what else can I do?"

Joan's husband and kids took over many of the household duties. Other parents in the neighborhood did more than their fair share of transporting the teens, hers and theirs, where they needed to go. "I'm grateful to them all," Joan thought, "but I hate how vulnerable I feel all the time."

After a particularly difficult day, she fell into a troubled sleep.

She had an intense dream in which she was yelling at the universe, demanding to know why she was being punished with this illness.

She heard a soft voice reply, "Actually, the illness is a gift. You need to learn to receive, and the illness is providing this opportunity."

Joan felt her heart stop. She needed to learn to receive? She had never even conceptualized this as a lesson one would need to learn.

She thought lessons were about giving — being able to give generously and lovingly. She had been a model of giving!

She still remembers the voice to this day.

"This is a gift for you and a gift for your family. Notice how you all have changed. You are learning to receive, and they are learning to give."

⌁

Receiving, for the good of all concerned, is divine.

⌁

To Give

Richard was out of work again. The economy was so bad that people weren't building homes. Construction had been his livelihood since high school. He was good at it and he liked it, but it certainly wasn't feeding his family these days. With bills mounting and money in short supply, he bid for any job he could find, but it wasn't enough. Times were tight.

In desperation, his wife Alison suggested they temporarily switch roles. She was pretty sure she could get her old teaching job back, but doing so would require him to stay home and care for their two small children. Richard saw no other way, so he agreed.

At first, staying home with the kids felt like a bad dream. "How did Alison do this?" he wondered. "It's so chaotic and there's so much to be done!"

After a while, though, the kids calmed down and became more used to their father's presence. And he developed a rhythm, just as he had done at the construction site. He figured out how to weave together care for them and the many chores and errands.

He found that he loved spending time with the kids. And he discovered that he loved creating an environment for his family in which they all thrived. He had not "given" in such a way before.

Richard is happy! Not only that, his wife Alison is happy, too. She realizes how much she had missed being in the work world. More important, she realizes what an amazing man her husband is, and is falling in love with him all over again.

Giving, for the good of all concerned, is divine.

Balance is the key. Balance — giving for the good of all concerned, and receiving for the good of all concerned...

The emphasis here is on "for the good of all concerned." It's not all about "you" and it's not all about "me." **It's about "us" — it's about win-win.**

Sometimes "for the good of all concerned" isn't as evident as it might be when all you can see is third base. You have to be able to see the larger picture — the whole ball game — to see how Joan's arthritis served everyone around her, and how Richard's difficulty in finding work to support his family served them all.

Approaching life with a philosophy that interactions will be mutually beneficial helps keep your giving and receiving positive and in balance.

Take you and me, for example. A win-win means that me giving to you, and you receiving from me, is positive for both of us — and vice versa.

However, this mutually beneficial approach may not be what you see every day. In what's characterized as a "dog-eat-dog" world, some individuals try to get as much as they can to make sure they and theirs are taken care of — often at the expense of others.

In their view, the quantity of resources is limited. They think there isn't enough power, money, food, or land to go around, so they take all they can.

You've seen this repeatedly in the news: Rich person gets even richer by paying low wages, raising prices, or cutting health insurance benefits.

This "scarcity" view of resources isn't accurate and is built on fear — the fear that comes about when you think third base is all there is. Remember, there is more to the ball game than what you can see with your physical eyes.

Another fear-based approach is when people try to be bigger and stronger than others so that no one can hurt them.

∽

Bully

Johnny was a bully. He had always been a bully.

In grade school he pushed kids around to show he was the toughest. In high school he did the same.

Now, as a manager of a large department store, he pushes around his employees. They fear him, and try to stay out of his way.

It all came to a head one day when a male employee didn't back down and do as Johnny ordered. In the intensity, Johnny shoved him.

Johnny is afraid. He deals with his fear by making those around him afraid of him.

That way he can have control of what occurs. Sometimes verbal badgering is sufficient to keep others under control.

Since this approach didn't work with the male employee, Johnny shoved him in order to maintain his position as the one doing the controlling.

This is the same behavior used by batterers in intimate relationships. Control is what they want. It's a way to assuage their fear.

Some in the "dog-eat-dog" or "bully" frame of mind fall into the trap of thinking they are more important than others.

Thus they think they deserve to "receive" more, no matter the cost.

Others fall into this trap, too. They think: "I am more important than you because of my job, my money, my ancestry, the country I live in, my ability to play football, etc."

The truth is that **no one person is more important than another.**

If you could see the entire ball game, the broader spiritual view, you would understand this with no doubts.

Monique's New Job

Monique's position in the agency was closer to the middle of the hierarchy than the top.

Shortly after starting work there she discovered that morale wasn't good.

People were tense and pressured. The boss, reactive by all accounts, often caused undue stress by flying off the handle before all the facts were on the table.

And some days were worse than others, depending on his mood. People didn't want to take things to him, for fear of his reaction and ultimate decision.

"Everyone around me is so stressed." Monique thought. "I don't want to work in this kind of environment."

So, she began to act the opposite of those around her. Instead of being stressed and heavy, she lightened the atmosphere with humor and an inner peacefulness.

Her co-workers appreciated this about her, and thankfully, over time, the lighter state spread to those she worked with.

When it came to conversations with the boss, she was smart. She assessed his mood and approached each meeting with respect, inner peacefulness, and when she could, humor. Over time, her boss gained respect for her. This made their interaction better, more effective. His respect allowed her more leeway in carrying out her job.

This has come to mean she can be more successful overall — in carrying out her work and in helping improve the work atmosphere for a lighter, better experience.

Monique's boss has a higher position in the company than she does, but that doesn't make him more important. Nor does it make his approach to life better than hers.

No one is more important than another. Everyone is of equal value.

Likewise, everyone can have an abundant life — you can have an abundant life full of love, security, joy and peace of mind.

The abundant life is a life of balance in giving and receiving for the good of all concerned.

This is equally true in all areas of your life — with people, animals, the Earth, and material goods.

This kind of equilibrium requires humility in equal proportion to self-esteem, and selflessness in equal proportion to self-interest.

Monique characterized these qualities. She wanted a good work environment for herself and others. She wanted a reasonable interaction with the boss for herself and for the benefit of the work that needed to be done. Monique also possessed the prerequisites for an abundant life — an awareness of, and a respect for, the world around her. She paid attention to what was happening at work and she took action with respect for all concerned.

What keeps you from an abundant life of giving and receiving?

You may have inaccurate core beliefs about yourself, the things you want, or the world in which you live. You are probably not consciously aware of all of these core beliefs. Thus, when you want things like peace of mind or more money, they don't materialize.

Likewise, if you want to be able to give in a particular way, it doesn't come to fruition. Your inaccurate core beliefs are short-circuiting your desires and abilities.

Inaccurate Core Beliefs
Possible core beliefs about yourself that keep you from achieving abundance — a balance of giving and receiving
I'm not worthy — *or* — I'm more worthy than you
I don't deserve it — *or* — I deserve more than you
I can't have it — *or* — I can have it but you can't
I can't get it right — *or* — I'm always right
I'm not important — *or* — I'm more important than you
I'm not smart enough — *or* — I am smarter than you

Inaccurate Core Beliefs	
Possible core beliefs about the things you want that keep you from appropriately receiving...	
Happiness	Life is hard and then you die.
	It's impossible to be happy in life.
	I don't deserve it.
	It's not okay to be happy when so many bad things are happening in the world.
	I have to suffer.

Inaccurate Core Beliefs	
Possible core beliefs about the things you want that keep you from appropriately receiving...	
Money	Other people can have it, but I can't.
	Wealthy people are greedy.
	Money corrupts.
	Money is the root of all evil.
	I do spiritual work, so I can't have money.
	I can only have a certain amount.
	I can't be rich.
	I don't deserve it.
	It's not okay to have money when so many other people don't have it.
Love	I am not lovable.
	I will be abandoned.
	I can't trust other people.
	Love is constraining and intrusive.
	I can't be myself, because the other person won't like me.

Inaccurate Core Beliefs
Possible core beliefs about the things you want that keep you from appropriately receiving...

Peace of mind	I have to be anxious and worry — it's the way one has to live in this world.
	Only spiritual leaders can have peace of mind.
	It takes years of meditation to achieve peace of mind.
	It is not possible.
	I don't deserve it.

Inaccurate Core Beliefs
Possible core beliefs that keep you from appropriately giving
If I give to you, you'll take advantage of me.
Others don't deserve what I have to give.
Why should I give? I deserve to receive.
Giving is not my job. My job is to take care of myself.
There isn't enough to go around, so I need to keep what I have.
"Survival of the fittest" is how the world works.
Giving makes me vulnerable.
It's all about me, not you.
I am more important than you, so you should give to me.
Taking care of the Earth is not my job.
My needs are more important than the negative effects on the environment.
I don't have time to consider your needs or the needs of the Earth.

Energy Field Disturbances

Energy field disturbances are obstacles that get in your way.

Energy Field Disturbances	
Fear	Inability to forgive yourself
Worry	Inability to forgive others
Doubt	Low self-esteem
Anger	Lack of faith
Unresolved issues	Lack of trust

These obstacles junk up your energy field. If you want a new relationship, for example, the relationship has to dodge all of the obstacles in the way before it can get to you.

These energy field disturbances are like shopping carts in a parking lot. Discarded shopping carts can junk up a parking lot so much that it's hard to find a place to park.

If you want to park, you have to stop, get out of the car, and remove any carts before you can pull in to a parking space.

Just like shopping carts, energy field disturbances need to be removed.

For example, the perfect relationship for you could be right before your eyes. You may see that you are attracted to someone, or even go out on a date or two.

However, if you fear the other person will take advantage of you, because this happened to you in a previous relationship, your fear of this happening again — your unresolved issue — could keep you from pursuing this new relationship further.

The fear and unresolved issue are the obstacles that you and the universe have to address in order to clear the path for the relationship you want.

Energy field disturbances also keep you from giving in the way you'd like. Your lack of trust in people, for example, may be an obstacle to your giving to them. Your lack of forgiveness of yourself or others could have the same effect, keeping you from giving and receiving.

The Law Of Attraction

What you believe, think, feel, and say becomes what you experience. You attract what you project out.

If you always think to yourself, "I'm in debt, I'm in debt, I'm in debt," you'll always be in debt. Or if you think, "I'm lonely, lonely, lonely," you'll be lonely.

Instead, think to yourself, "I have the money I need to pay the bills." Imagine yourself paying off your bills. Envision more resources than bills. These thoughts will "attract" this experience of paying off your bills.

In order to attract social interaction, think to yourself, "I have many friends and loved ones. We enjoy one another's company and do fun things together." Envision the time you spend together. Picture the social activities you participate in. These thoughts will "attract" these experiences.

Be sure to be clear about what it is that you want for your life, and know that the best timing for all concerned may not be what you originally had in mind.

But don't give up!

Now take a closer look at yourself — both at your strengths and at the ways you'd like to improve your giving and receiving.

Giving and Receiving
What things do you receive well?
What keeps you from receiving all that you want?

Giving and Receiving
In what ways do you give well?
What keeps you from giving in the ways you want?

Giving and receiving, for the good of **all** concerned, is divine. It's a win-win. And it usually feels good, too.

Giving to others is an important part of your journey. Giving does not mean giving yourself away, however. In domestic violence situations for example, batterers try to gain and maintain control of the other person. The person being battered may give themselves away to what the batterer wants in order to maintain a semblance of peace in the household.

This is beyond giving. It's bad for the one being controlled and battered because that person loses themselves in the process. And it's bad for the batterer because this behavior makes everyone, including the abuser, unhappy and unsafe. Professional intervention is needed.

In addition, it's bad for the children, because they learn the "controller/controlled" behavior. Abuse is not acceptable in any way. It is a lose-lose all the way around.

Giving and receiving for the good of all concerned — including you — is divine. Giving to others should feel good. And receiving from others should feel good. Remember Yessenia and Gloria in Chapter Two? Yessenia had a flat tire and Gloria and Juan stopped to help her. Everyone felt good in that interaction. Plus, Yessenia and Gloria became good friends.

Remember, living life is a matter of balance. This isn't the "walking a tightrope" kind of balance. It's the kind of balance required to stay on your side of the roadway — which is simply a matter of respecting all that is around you and taking actions that are for the good of all concerned.

We have so much yet to achieve in this world. Read on to discover exciting new adventures ahead for you and humankind! We haven't even begun to reach the peak of possibility!

Chapter 7

Mistake #7 —
Thinking Humankind
Has Already Reached Its Peak

Do you wonder if there's anything new to discover? If there is anything new to do?

Have you heard anyone say the world is coming to an end?

Do you remember the Y2K fuss at the end of 1999 over the coming of the year 2000? People were preparing for the worst as we entered the new millennium.

With war continuing on our planet, the persistence of hunger and disease, and the pollution of our resources, some assert that humankind already reached its peak and it's only downhill from here.

Have we reached our peak?

Are we there yet?

Not exactly.

This would be the point in the journey where the parents engage the children in the license plate game, distracting them from the next question of "How much longer?"

We are not there yet, and there's a bit of distance to go. We can "be" so much more than we currently are.

Every generation seems to think it has achieved everything there is to achieve. Yet lo and behold, the next generation brings even more fantastic inventions and understandings.

∽

Clara, 1900–1992

"We thought we were "the cat's meow" when Daddy took us for a ride in our very first car! It was thrilling! We rode all the way through town and got to wave to all of our friends!"

Anna loved it when her grandmother, Clara, told stories like this. Anna remembered how her grandmother shook her head in amazement at what she'd seen during her life.

The Wright brothers made the first flight in an airplane in 1903, the same year that Edward Binney and Harold Smith invented crayons. "Childhood without crayons?" Anna thought. She couldn't imagine it.

Shortly afterwards Albert Einstein published his Theory of Relativity. The Ford Model T automobile was first sold in 1908 and Thomas Edison demonstrated the first talking motion picture in 1910.

Anna laughed when her grandmother told her that Band-Aids were invented in 1920. "What did they do before Band-Aids?" Anna wondered.

Insulin was invented in 1922 and penicillin was discovered in 1928.

Her grandmother reminded Anna to pay attention to what was coming into the world.

Anna is 30 now, and has already witnessed many new inventions: home computers, the Internet, cordless telephones, video games, cell phones, navigation systems, fax machines, home copy machines, CDs, DVDs, MP3s...

Anna credits her grandmother for helping her appreciate these amazing new developments. Her awareness of these new things coming into being helps her to have hope for the future.

Given all that's behind us, can you imagine what's ahead? It is beyond what any of us can imagine. This is because one understanding is built on another, and another, and another, until things are further out than you can even begin to conceptualize.

Corey the Writer

"What's the use?" Corey thought. "The world's going to hell in a hand-basket and there's nothing I can do about it. Anything I have to say has already been said or already been written, and no one's paying attention anyway!"

Corey was becoming more depressed with each passing day. In his misery, he caught a cold, then the flu. Alternating between fever and chills, he slipped into delirium. He felt like he was hurtling through the universe.

No longer in touch with his ailing physical body, he found himself on a planet, looking at a field of crops.

"Where am I?" he thought. "On future Earth," he heard. "The soil and plants are infused with the nutrients they need to grow healthy food. 'Infusing' is a technique that was developed over time, to counteract the depletion of the soil and eliminate the need for chemical additives."

Corey was surprised. He had presumed food would become more and more chemical and artificial, until crops weren't even grown any more.

"Who are you?" Corey asked.

Ellery stepped forward and smiled. "I am a future descendant of yours. I'll be your guide while you're here. Let me show you around."

Corey saw communities and schools and health centers. "It's so quiet and clean." Corey remarked. Ellery explained, "Coal and oil aren't used as energy sources much any more. The sun and air are our primary energies."

"People look so healthy."

"Yes," Ellery said. "Through medical and psychological science, we've learned more about the human energy field. This is the field of energy in and around your body. We've learned it is key in preventing and treating disease. Your energy field can become clogged with emotional issues and mental misperceptions, which then cause physical problems. Understanding this relationship has revolutionized health care.

"What about war?" Corey asked. "Are we at war with each other?"

"Some war still exists," Ellery said, "but it's the exception, not the rule. And soon, it will only be a distant memory of what we used to do before we learned better ways to live together in this world."

"What you're showing me is so hard to believe," Corey said. "On present Earth, it looks like we're heading in an entirely different direction."

"A small group of thoughtful people can change the world. Indeed, it is the only thing that ever has." This quote of Margaret Mead's went round and round in Corey's head as he awoke in his bed at home.

Don't give up!

If you look through lenses of abundance, you'll see individuals and organizations that are working throughout the world for positive change. You see people giving of themselves for humankind.

There are over 100 international charities doing just that today, such as Habitat for Humanity, Doctors without Borders, the International Red Cross, and Amnesty International. These people are making a difference. These people have not accepted that humankind has reached its peak.

Spiritually, people are discovering their connection with Source… a Higher Power… God. A void is being filled as spiritual centers are experiencing a renewed interest.

If you believe the world has peaked, then your vision for today is influenced by this limiting thought.

This is an energetic understanding of how the universe operates. There has been much emphasis on the physical and material aspects of understanding life recently. This leaves much room for re-engaging in the energetic and spiritual arenas. Some are exploring new thought and experience that are based on ancient wisdom — the wisdom of those who have come before you.

How would you like to see the world develop?

How would you like to see yourself develop?

How about internal peace?

How about the mindfulness to allow each moment to unfold? This approach eliminates worry and anxiety, because you're not projecting into the future or falling back into the past. What a gift this would be!

How about the expansiveness to connect and communicate with your loved ones who have passed on? Connect and communicate with them as easily as your next-door neighbors, allowing you to continue as significant parts of each other's daily lives.

~

The Hypnotist's Newsletter

Let's see, it's been three weeks since my last confession...

Wait, that's not quite it... It's been three weeks since my last newsletter.

Or has it been three lifetimes? It's easy to be confused about three weeks or three lifetimes when you've just finished a past-life regression class. This is where all those folks who had such a good time learning to be hypnotists get to learn how to use hypnotism to regress people to past lives.

Featuring such activities as the "Come As You Were" party, it's a ball of fun.

There were eight of us. We spent six days being regressed into past lives or regressing others, sprawled all over the floor (you have to be comfortable, after all, and those hard-backed chairs just didn't do it.) Each of us was regressed back to one or two past lives every day. It's an interesting thing, learning about the past lives of people before you know much about who they are in their current life. Somehow it worked, though, as the past lives always had something to do with their current life. Through the unraveling of the past, we learned about each other's current lives.

Take me for example. I've experienced a lot of spiritual development this year; not surprisingly, most of the past lives I regressed to were somehow linked to this.

I had one life where I was a teenager in the jungles of South America. I remember so clearly being young and thin and absolutely loving, loving, loving to run.

I was the one sent to neighboring villages miles away to deliver messages. The experience of filling my lungs with oxygen as I ran was intoxicating. I grew up in this life, mated, had children, and became an old man.

The amazing thing about the village I lived in was that it was very spiritual.

When village members passed on, they remained a significant part of our lives. When my father passed on, I still talked with him everyday and he talked with me. The only differences were that he was not in physical form and he had access to a much larger view of life.

This communication, this closeness, with those who had passed on was simply part of our everyday lives. We were taught as children how to live and communicate in this way.

One of my last significant memories in that life was just before I passed on. I was talking with my grandchildren about how it would be to communicate with me when I was no longer in physical form.

While not all of the students in the past-life regression class actually believed in past lives when they started the class, we were all believers by the end.

Who might you be at the "Come As You Were" party?

Positive change is possible and probable at every level. And even what seems like significant change won't take long. Each new understanding multiplies in effect, bringing the next understanding even faster.

Have you reached your peak? Not even close. Possibility is infinite.

So why don't you see and feel this infinite possibility? It goes back to some of what we talked about in the last chapter — inaccurate core beliefs and energy field disturbances. Inaccurate core beliefs limit what you think is possible. Similarly, energy field disturbances like fear and doubt hold you back. They are obstacles that have to be learned so that your life's possibility can be realized.

Remember Angela from Chapter Three? Here's another of the entries in her diary.

Angela's Diary Entry

I've just returned home after a lovely time at the beach. My usual — a run and the coffee shop. I had been reading — well, actually, reading is too strong a word... I had been skimming sections of a book about health and fitness. I was hoping to pick up some pointers.

Instead, the book helped me to realize that an issue I've been struggling with is all about fear. I need to let go of the fear!

Then and there I asked for help letting go of the fear in my life: "Whatever it takes, for the good of all concerned, help me let go of the fear."

This was no small request, but it was fuelled by the substantial reduction in fear I've experienced these past many months. Life with less fear looks and feels entirely different. I'm much happier, and I'm ready to go the distance. If I can experience less fear, why not no fear at all?

When I arrived home I was distracted immediately, in close proximity to the many things that needed attention. I found myself saying, "Wait a minute, my job at this moment is to get in the shower, take my vitamins, and let go of all fear." I laughed. Oh yes. "Let go of all fear." That little thing.

It reminded me of a series of cards some friends sent me. Almost 25 years later, I still have them.

Card 1: A woman stands at a street corner, waiting for the light to change. In her thought bubble: "Think positively, stop worrying, be myself, take a risk, be open with people, don't slouch, figure out what I really want to do with my life, be more assertive, start my diet... Now I know there's something else I'm supposed to do today..."

Card 2: A woman shoveling dirt into a large hole. "Mad woman trying to bury delicate feelings once and for all!"

Card 3: A woman doing dishes, looking out her kitchen window at a tree. "Gazing out the window while rinsing the morning dishes, she chased her thoughts in circles, until they escaped through the screen and onto the mulberry tree. From a distance, they actually made sense."

Card 4: A woman looking in the mirror, saying to herself, "Change, damn it, change!"

I am alternately each and every one of these women. The real question is, though, who do I want to be? A woman without fear. A woman who experiences at least as much growth this year as in this last life-changing year.

I put the question out to the universe. "How do I continue the growth and change?" The answer I received is that the way to growth, positive change, is opening. Life presents endless opportunities for opening — opening our minds, opening our hearts, opening our perspectives, opening our experiences, opening our feelings, opening our spirits… Opening!

"But what about the pain?" I asked. "Pain seems to be a prerequisite for the opening required in growth." The reply came — opening does not need to be painful, though sometimes it is pain that finally motivates us to open. Opening is required. Pain is optional.

Card 5: All of us gathered, hearts beating strong and hands clasping hands, as we open, open, open to the profound growth of the New Year!

Have you reached your peak? Not even close. Possibility is infinite.

What growth and change would you like for yourself?	What growth and change would you like for the world?

This would be the point in the journey where the parents check that the seat belts are securely buckled, put the top down, and make time. Hold on to your hats!

Remember, you haven't even seen the peak of your possibility yet. You can "be" so much more than you currently are. Keep learning, keep growing, keep seeking.

The next chapter sums it all up, so read on for a recap of your Spiritual Home Field Advantage.

Chapter 8

7 Critical Understandings to Retain

1. *Remember,* **it would be impossible to overestimate the power of love and connection. Love and connection are the heart of your well-being. Open your heart and you have everything. Live life for the love of it!**

Fully engage with life. Be fully present. Care. Love. Be passionate about what's important to you. Do what you love. Be what you love. Be fully you! Being open-hearted and thus fully you is the safest and most fulfilling approach to life. This is because a closed heart leads to separation — from yourself and others.

Not being in full connection with yourself and others requires you to live life in a limited way. It allows you to make choices that are not the best for you, such as accepting a job or a relationship that doesn't fulfill you. Likewise, you can feel alone or afraid in this world because you're not in full connection.

Live life fully — for the love of it and for the love of you.

2. *Remember,* there's generally more to the story than meets the eye… the physical eye, that is. So turn your eye to the broader perspective of the spiritual realm to understand what life's situations are really about.

This is true for everything, whether it's a broken computer, parenting problems, or feelings of anxiety. Trying to understand and live life from a physical world perspective is like trying to understand the game of baseball by watching only the third baseman — your perspective isn't broad enough, so what's happening doesn't fully make sense.

Think of your physical life as a field trip. Most of your existence, your eons and eons of existence, is lived at "Home" in the spiritual realm.

You have physical lives — field trips — so that you can learn and contribute in specific ways. Thus, when things happen in your physical life, they happen for a purpose.

Everything happens for a purpose.

For example, losing your job may be just what you need in order to be pointed in a different direction — a direction that will be more helpful to you and all concerned in achieving all that you came here to achieve.

3. *Remember,* you are not alone — never have been, never will be. Your loved ones are with you whether you, or they, are in physical form or spirit form. They are with you forever and they are with you always.

At "Home" in the spiritual realm, you have a very large family of loved ones. Some of these loved ones come with you on your field trip to Earth.

Perhaps you've had the experience of feeling a strong connection to someone you just met. It's because you knew them at "Home."

Some of your loved ones who don't come with you on your Earth field trip volunteer to help you while you're here.

This is your Spiritual Home Field Advantage.

Everyone in spirit form knows how challenging it can be in this physical world, so you're sent here with guides and teachers.

Your spirit guides help you navigate this physical realm so that you can accomplish all that you set forth to accomplish.

This includes nudging you in various ways when you need to change directions.

4. *Remember,* **there is no chance that life is left to chance. Some of it is planned and some of it is left up to your free will.**

Use the guidance you receive to effectively navigate the physical world so that you might achieve all that you came to achieve.

Before you came into this world, you determined what it is was that you wanted to accomplish while here.

You then worked with your advisors in the spiritual realm to develop circumstances in this physical life that would allow for the opportunities you needed to accomplish these things.

When life appears to throw you a curve ball, it is actually throwing you one of these opportunities.

Some aspects of our lives are planned, like the presenting of these opportunities.

At the same time, we have free will — we make choices about how we lead our physical lives. Our job is to step up to the plate and take responsibility for how we live our lives.

5. *Remember,* your life is of tremendous consequence to you and to all of existence. This is because we're all connected. Every thought you have, every action you take, impacts everything else — everything that exists.

Every bit of your learning and development makes it easier for others to learn and develop. Each act of kindness, each act of love, has an impact. It helps you and everyone else in the quest to learn, contribute, and evolve. You are everything, and everything is you.

You have purpose in being here. Each one of us has purpose. There are the visible Mother Teresas, and there are those that are not so visible — each with equally important purposes.

You have a critical role to play in this baseball game of life. Sometimes it's hard to know, because you can often only see third base.

If you could see the whole ball game — the broader view through a spiritual lens — you would better understand your critical role.

What may appear to you to be insignificant actions or events may actually be of great significance.

Our lives are interrelated, like drops of water in the ocean. We're each here for our own journey as well as the journeys of others. We're all in this together!

6. *Remember,* living life is a matter of balance. This isn't about the "walking a tightrope" kind of balance. It's the kind of balance required to stay on your side of the roadway — simply a matter of respecting all that is around you and taking actions that are for the good of all concerned.

No one person is more important than another. Everyone is of equal value. Everyone can have an abundant life. You can have an abundant life — love, security, joy and peace of mind.

The abundant life is a life of balance in giving and receiving for the good of all concerned. This is equally true in all areas of your life — with people, animals, the Earth, and material goods.

This kind of equilibrium requires humility in equal proportion to self-esteem, and selflessness in equal proportion to self-interest.

7. Remember, **you haven't even seen the peak of your possibility yet. You can "be" so much more than you currently are. Keep learning, keep growing, keep seeking.**

Every generation seems to think it has achieved what there is to achieve; yet lo and behold, the next generation brings even more fantastic inventions and understandings.

Given all that's behind us, can you imagine what's ahead? It is beyond what any of us can imagine.

This is because one understanding is built on another, and another, and another, until things are further out than you could even begin to conceptualize.

Positive change is possible and probable at every level. And the fact is, even what seems like significant change won't take long.

Each new understanding multiplies in effect, bringing the next understanding even faster.

Have you reached your peak?

Not even close. Possibility is infinite!